For ....

From ....

Date ....

D1531749

HUNDREDS OF HEARTWARMING QUOTES

A Mother's Love

Beautiful, Unconditional, ... and Forever

Adamsmedia

AVON, MASSACHUSETTS

Copyright © 2017 by F+W Media, Inc.
All rights reserved.
This book, or parts thereof, may not be reproduced in any form without permission from
the publisher; exceptions are made for brief excerpts used in published reviews.

Published by
Adams Media, a division of F+W Media, Inc.
57 Littlefield Street, Avon, MA 02322. U.S.A.
www.adamsmedia.com

Contains material adapted from *All about Mom*, edited by Dahlia Porter
and Gabriel Cervantes, copyright © 2006 by F+W Media, Inc.,
ISBN 10: 1-59337-599-9, ISBN 13: 978-1-59337-599-7.

ISBN 10: 1-5072-0113-3
ISBN 13: 978-1-5072-0113-8
eISBN 10: 1-5072-0114-1
eISBN 13: 978-1-5072-0114-5

Printed in the United States of America.

10   9   8   7   6   5   4   3   2   1

Many of the designations used by manufacturers and sellers to distinguish their products are
claimed as trademarks. Where those designations appear in this book and F+W Media, Inc.,
was aware of a trademark claim, the designations have been printed with initial capital letters.

Cover design by Stephanie Hannus.
Cover and interior images © Karma15381/Getty Images.

This book is available at quantity discounts for bulk purchases.
For information, please call 1-800-289-0963.

Introduction

Mothers are the glue that holds our hearts together.

From the second your children are born, you are their greatest advocate, most sympathetic friend, and greatest ally. Your unconditional love is with your children all the time—and it appears in many forms. A hug, a text, a batch of their favorite cookies . . . no one's love is quite like a mom's.

In these quotes, you will find love, appreciation, and praise. You'll find humor and joy. You may also find heartbreak and even anger. Through the pages of this book, bits and pieces of thousands of human emotions swirl around, and there stands Mom at the center of it all. After all, a mother is "a hurricane in its perfect power," as Maya Angelou says.

If there's one common thread among these quotes, it is gratitude. Behind everything from Mark Twain's crafty witticisms to NBA star Kevin Durant's basketball analogies to J.K. Rowling's beautifully woven web of love and magic, there is one echo: "Thank you, Mom, for everything that you are."

It's the one job where, the better you are,
the more surely you won't be needed
in the long run.

BARBARA KINGSOLVER, WRITER

Yes, Mother . . . I can see
you are flawed. You have
not hidden it. That is your
greatest gift to me.

ALICE WALKER, WRITER , POET, AND ACTIVIST

The walks and talks we have with our two-year-olds in red boots have a great deal to do with the values they will cherish as adults.

ᎦᏉ EDITH F. HUNTER, WRITER ᎦᏉ

Love as powerful as your mother's for you leaves its own mark . . . to have been loved so deeply . . . will give us some protection forever.

ᎦᏉ J.K. ROWLING, WRITER ᎦᏉ

Advice to mothers: Take off your earrings, your ring, your precious family heirloom, and give them to [your daughter], along with your love and trust. Trust and love are wonderful, but don't forget the earrings.

᷐ ESTÉE LAUDER, BUSINESSWOMAN ᷐

I remember my mother's prayers and they have always followed me. They have clung to me all my life.

ABRAHAM LINCOLN, 16TH PRESIDENT OF THE UNITED STATES

Being a mother, as far as I can tell,
is a constantly evolving process of
adapting to the needs of your child
while also changing and growing as
a person in your own right.

တ DEBORAH INSEL, WRITER ည

Over the years, I learned so much from mom. She taught me about the importance of home and history and family and tradition. She also taught me that aging need not mean narrowing the scope of your activities and interests or a diminution of the *great pleasures* to be had in the everyday.

∽ MARTHA STEWART, BUSINESSWOMAN ∾

My mother was the one constant in my life. When I think about my mom raising me alone when she was 20, and working and paying the bills, and, you know, trying to pursue your own dreams, I think is a feat that is unmatched.

ﻌﻌ BARACK OBAMA, 44TH PRESIDENT OF THE UNITED STATES ﻌﻌ

My mother was the source from which I derived the guiding principles of my life.

ᴓᴚ JOHN WESLEY, THEOLOGIAN ᴚᴓ

Acceptance, tolerance, bravery, compassion. These are the things my mom taught me.

ᴓᴚ LADY GAGA, MUSICIAN ᴚᴓ

I am all the time talking about you, and bragging, to
one person or another. I am like the Ancient Mariner,
who had a tale in his heart he must unfold to all.
I am always button-holing somebody and saying,
"Someday you must meet my mother." And then
I am off. And nothing stops me till the waiters close
up the café. I do love you so much, my mother. . . .
If I didn't keep calling you mother, anybody reading
this would think I was writing to my sweetheart.
And he would be quite right.

EDNA ST. VINCENT MILLAY, POET AND PLAYWRIGHT

She drove me to ballet class . . . and she took me to every audition. She'd be proud of me if I was still sitting in that seat or if I was watching from home. She believes in me and that's why this [award] is for her. She's a wonderful mother.

ၼ ELISABETH MOSS, ACTRESS ၼ

I've never been this exhausted.
No matter how much I played, I knew
that in soccer I'd get one day off a week,
I'd get some weeks off once in a while.
Here, they don't care. They don't care if
it's a holiday. Sleep in—what's that?

๛ MIA HAMM, PROFESSIONAL SOCCER PLAYER ๛

If the whole world were put into one scale,
and my mother in the other,
the whole world would kick the beam.

๛ HENRY BICKERSTETH, LORD LANGDALE, LAW REFORMER ๛

It seems to me that my mother was the most splendid woman I ever knew. . . . I have met a lot of people knocking around the world since, but I have never met a more thoroughly refined woman than my mother. If I have amounted to anything, it will be due to her.

CHARLIE CHAPLIN, ACTOR, DIRECTOR, AND COMPOSER

I am very protective. I just want to make sure that she can have a healthy, safe, normal life . . . in the back of my mind, she's my priority. And life is completely different now. I feel *really, really* just lucky that I can still do what I love, and now have a way bigger meaning.
And that's to be her mother.

∽ BEYONCÉ, MUSICIAN ∾

Whatever beauty or poetry is to be found in my little book is owing to your interest in and encouragement of all my efforts from the first to the last; and if ever I do anything to be proud of, my greatest happiness will be that I can thank you for that, as I may do for all the good there is in me; and I shall be content to write if it gives you pleasure.

⚜ LOUISA MAY ALCOTT, WRITER, IN A LETTER TO HER MOTHER ⚜

Motherhood is tough. If you just want
a wonderful little creature to love,
you can get a puppy.

࿔ BARBARA WALTERS, WRITER AND JOURNALIST ࿔

[My mother] gave me the example of the completely
dedicated life. In my father this was translated into
action, and in my mother into silence. We all live from
what woman has taught us of the sublime.

࿔ POPE PAUL VI ࿔

My mother taught me how to love. My mom is the most loving person I know.

ഛ CHANNING TATUM, ACTOR ൭

Motherhood is priced
Of God, at price no man may dare
To lessen or misunderstand.

ഛ HELEN HUNT JACKSON, WRITER AND ACTIVIST ൭

The fastest way to break the cycle of perfectionism and become a fearless mother is to give up the idea of doing it perfectly—indeed to embrace uncertainty and imperfection.

ARIANNA HUFFINGTON, BUSINESSWOMAN

You are like an everlasting friendship. You are like a secret almost too wonderful to keep. You are like the beginning, end, and everything in between. You are like a spring shower. You are like the sun shining on me and keeping me warm. You are like a wild flower in the meadow. You are like a very knowledgeable volume of encyclopedias. You are like you and I love you.

LAUREL O. HOYE, POET, AGE EIGHT, TO HER MOTHER

I . . . have another cup of coffee with my mother. We get along very well, veterans of a guerrilla war we never understood.

Ͼᵒᵉ JOAN DIDION, WRITER Ͽᵉᵃ

And (cue music swell) motherhood turned out to be the most meaningful thing I've ever done with my life. Really.

Ͼᵒᵉ NIA VARDALOS, ACTRESS Ͽᵉᵃ

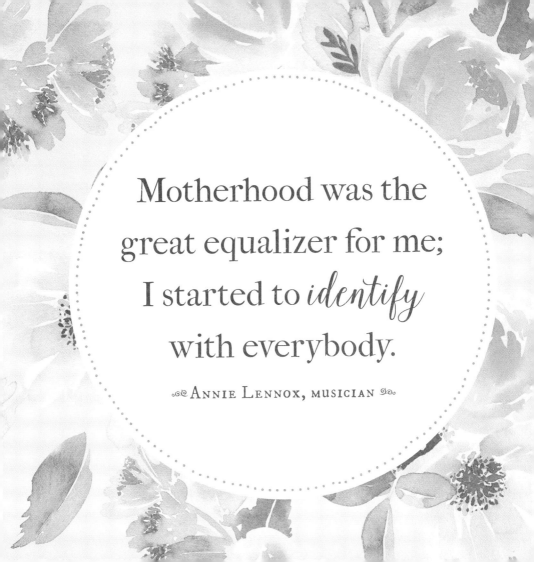

Motherhood was the great equalizer for me; I started to *identify* with everybody.

∞ ANNIE LENNOX, MUSICIAN ∞

There were times when, in middle school and junior high, I didn't have a lot of friends. But my mom was always my friend. Always.

ఴ TAYLOR SWIFT, MUSICIAN ఴ

A mother is a mother still,
the holiest thing alive.

Ꙩ SAMUEL TAYLOR COLERIDGE, POET Ꙩ

I am aglow with the rapture of the revelation
that she is the most beautiful thing
in the whole world, my mother.

Ꙩ ADELE WISEMAN, WRITER Ꙩ

By no amount of agile exercising of a wistful imagination could my mother have been called lenient. Generous she was; indulgent, never. Kind, yes; permissive, never. In her world, people she accepted paddled their own canoes, pulled their own weight, put their own shoulders to their own plows and pushed like hell.

৩৫ MAYA ANGELOU, POET ৫৩

My mother phones daily to ask,
"Did you just try to reach me?" When I reply,
"No," she adds, "So if you're not too busy,
call me while I'm still alive," and hangs up.

৵৹ ERMA BOMBECK, HUMORIST ৹৵

My mother had a great deal
of trouble with me but
I think she enjoyed it.

৵৹ MARK TWAIN, WRITER ৹৵

Even if I say my mother was mean, I *still love her* and anyhow she wasn't that mean. I exaggerate everything I fear.

ANNE SEXTON, POET, TO HER DAUGHTER

One day my mother called me . . .
and she said, "Forty-nine million
Americans saw you on television tonight.
One of them is the father of my future
grandchild, but he's never going to call
you because you wore your glasses."

∽ LESLEY STAHL, JOURNALIST ∾

Motherhood: All love begins
and ends there.

∽ ROBERT BROWNING, POET ∾

The phrase "working mother"
is redundant.

ᕯ JANE SELLMAN, WRITER ᕯ

Whatever success comes to me seems
incomplete because you are so often not
at my side to be glad with me.

ᕯ HELEN KELLER, ACTIVIST, IN A LETTER TO HER MOTHER ᕯ

Motherhood definitely took the focus off of my work. And I didn't mind.

တေUMA THURMAN, ACTRESS ၅၀

There will be so many times you feel like you've failed. But in the eyes, heart, and mind of your child, you ARE Super Mom.

တေSTEPHANIE PRECOURT, WRITER ၅၀

In all my efforts to learn to read my mother shared fully my ambition, and sympathized with me and aided me in every way that she could.... If I have done anything in life worth attention, I feel sure that I inherited the disposition from my mother.

∽ BOOKER T. WASHINGTON, POLITICAL ADVISOR ∼

Motherhood has helped me to stop overanalyzing things. It's been liberating because I used to be somewhat neurotic. I attribute that to having something bigger than myself.

∾◦ IDINA MENZEL, ACTRESS AND SINGER ◦∾

Mother is the name for God in the lips and hearts of little children.

∾◦ WILLIAM MAKEPEACE THACKERAY, NOVELIST ◦∾

Every mother is like Moses.
She does not enter the promised land.
She prepares a world she will not see.

ഇൻ POPE PAUL VI ഉൻ

Mom, I love you and I thank you for what
you did for me, but I'll never tell you,
so I'll have to put it in a song.

ഇൻ GARTH BROOKS, MUSICIAN ഉൻ

Motherhood is neither a duty nor a privilege, but simply the way that humanity can satisfy the desire for physical immortality and triumph over the fear of death.

പ്റREBECCA WEST, WRITER ൨ൟ

I think motherhood is just about instinct.

പ്റKOURTNEY KARDASHIAN, TELEVISION PERSONALITY ൨ൟ

Motherhood was my career. I'm totally satisfied with that.

೭ ANN ROMNEY, FORMER FIRST LADY OF MASSACHUSETTS ೨

Blushing, full of confusion, I talked with her about my worries and the fear in my body. I fell on her breast, and all over again I became a little girl sobbing in her arms at the terror of life.

೭ GABRIELA MISTRAL, POET AND DIPLOMAT, IN "MOTHER" ೨

Life *began* with
waking up and loving
my mother's face.

⋙ GEORGE ELIOT, NOVELIST AND POET ⋘

To her whose heart is my heart's quiet home, To my first Love, my Mother, on whose knee I learnt love-lore that is not troublesome.

CHRISTINA ROSSETTI, POET

You count the hours you could have spent with your mother, it's a lifetime in itself.

MITCH ALBOM, WRITER

Motherhood has completely changed me. It's just about like the most completely humbling experience that I've ever had. I think that it puts you in your place because it really forces you to address the issues that you claim to believe in and if you can't stand up to those principles when you're raising a child, forget it.

∽ DIANE KEATON, ACTRESS ∾

Ah! what a joy is it to be able to turn in full confidence to the one whom we have to thank for our existence.

 જ FREDRIKA BREMER, WRITER AND REFORMER જ

When Jack Burns needed to hold his mother's hand, his fingers could see in the dark.

 જ JOHN IRVING, WRITER જ

Motherhood has a very humanizing effect. Everything gets reduced to essentials.

MERYL STREEP, ACTRESS

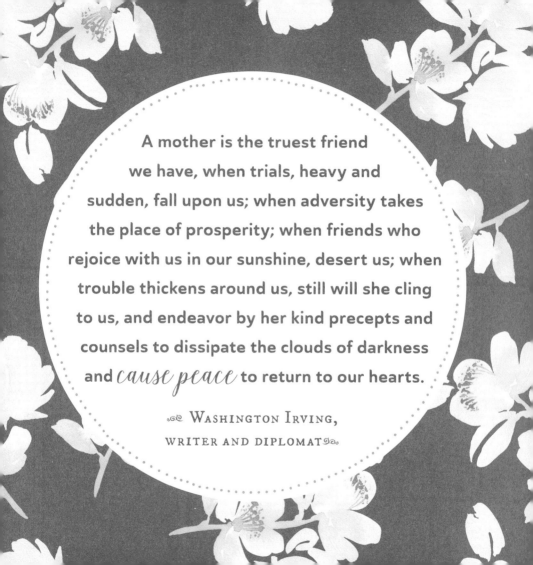

A mother is the truest friend we have, when trials, heavy and sudden, fall upon us; when adversity takes the place of prosperity; when friends who rejoice with us in our sunshine, desert us; when trouble thickens around us, still will she cling to us, and endeavor by her kind precepts and counsels to dissipate the clouds of darkness and *cause peace* to return to our hearts.

∞ WASHINGTON IRVING,
WRITER AND DIPLOMAT ∞

My mother . . . she is beautiful,
softened at the edges and
tempered with a spine of steel.
I want to grow old and be like her.

ଉକ JODI PICOULT, WRITER ୭ୟ

Having children just puts the
whole world into perspective.
Everything else just disappears.

ଉକ KATE WINSLET, ACTRESS ୭ୟ

I want to lean into her
the way wheat leans
into wind.

◦◦ LOUISE ERDRICH, WRITER ◦◦

The heart of a mother is a deep abyss at the bottom
of which you will always find forgiveness.

◦◦ HONORÉ DE BALZAC, NOVELIST AND PLAYWRIGHT ◦◦

Grown don't mean nothing to a mother. A child is a child. They get bigger, older, but grown? What's that supposed to mean? In my heart it don't mean a thing.

ஃ TONI MORRISON, WRITER ஃ

Who ran to help me when I fell,
And would some pretty story tell,
Or kiss the place to make it well?
My mother.

ஃ ANN TAYLOR, POET ஃ

I want my children to have all the things I couldn't afford. Then I want to move in with them.

ᴘʜʏʟʟɪꜱ ᴅɪʟʟᴇʀ, ᴀᴄᴛʀᴇꜱꜱ ᴀɴᴅ ᴄᴏᴍᴇᴅɪᴀɴ

In the beginning there was my mother. A shape. A shape and a force, standing in the light. You could see her energy; it was visible in the air. Against any background she stood out.

◦◦ MARILYN KRYSL, WRITER ◦◦

When I broke from modeling, it felt wonderful because I stopped thinking of myself as a pretty face. If I take time off from acting for motherhood, my life will deepen in the same way. I feel as if I've got my membership now in an exclusive club and I plan on enjoying it. Acting can wait.

∽ ANDIE MACDOWELL, ACTRESS ∽

I wonder why you care so much about me—
no, I don't wonder. I only accept it as the
thing at the back of all one's life that
makes everything bearable and possible.

ଶ୧ GERTRUDE BELL, BRITISH WRITER, ARCHAEOLOGIST,
AND SPY, IN A LETTER TO HER MOTHER ଶ୭

But if you've ever had a mother,
and if she's given you and meant
to you all the things you care
for most, you never get over it.

ଶ୧ ANNE DOUGLAS SEDGWICK, WRITER ଶ୭

There's constantly people asking you for something, so the multitasking of motherhood transfers very well to being a director. And, I think, you're compassionate.

◈ ANGELINA JOLIE, ACTRESS ◈

As mothers and daughters, we are *connected* with one another. My mother is the bones of my spine, keeping me straight and true. She is my blood, making sure it runs rich and strong. She is the beating of my heart. I cannot now imagine a life without her.

KRISTIN HANNAH, WRITER

To Love the tender heart hath ever fled,
As on its mother's breast the infant throws
Its sobbing face, and there in sleep forgets its woes.

⚮ MARY TIGHE, POET ⚭

My love for her is greater than my
love for the game that has made me
independently wealthy, and to which
I owe all I now possess.

⚮ BENNY LEONARD, PROFESSIONAL BOXER ⚭

From my earliest days she always had all the love and care I needed; I cannot recall that I ever felt she had been inadequate when my demands on her were emotional rather than practical.

∽ JONATHAN YARDLEY, BOOK CRITIC, OF HIS MOTHER ∾

Even as a very small child, I understood that women had secrets, and that some of these were only to be told to daughters. In this way we were bound together for eternity.

∽ ALICE HOFFMAN, WRITER ∾

There's no doubt that
motherhood is the
best thing in my life.
It's all that really matters.

࿐ COURTNEY COX, ACTRESS࿐

How beautifully everything is
arranged by Nature; as soon as
a child enters the world, it finds a
mother ready to take care of it.

࿐ JULES MICHELET, HISTORIAN࿐

"I always wondered why God was supposed to be a father," she whispers. "Fathers always want you to measure up to something. Mothers are the ones who love you unconditionally, don't you think?"

JODI PICOULT, WRITER

Mother, in ways neither of us can ever understand, I have come home.

ROBIN MORGAN, WRITER

Mother—that was the bank where we deposited all our hurts and worries.

ఆ T. DeWitt Talmage, preacher ఆ

There is no way to be a perfect mother, and a million ways to be a good one.

ఆ Jill Churchill, writer ఆ

I grow old, old without you, Mother, landscape of my heart.

ᆱ OLGA BROUMAS, POET ᕲ

[What's beautiful about my mother is] her compassion, how much she gives, whether it be to her kids and grandkids or out in the world. She's got a sparkle.

ᆱ KATE HUDSON, ACTRESS ᕲ

Motherhood . . . is a choice you make every day, to put someone else's happiness and well-being ahead of your own, to teach the hard lessons, to do the right thing even when you're not sure what the right thing is . . . and to *forgive yourself,* over and over again, for doing everything wrong.

≈∙∙ DONNA BALL, WRITER ∙∙≈

I think **every working mom probably feels the same thing: You go through big chunks of time where you're just thinking, "This is impossible—oh, this is impossible." And then you just keep going and keep going, and you sort of do the impossible.**

அ◦TINA FEY, ACTRESS ◦ை

There is eternal influence and power in motherhood.

அ◦ANONYMOUS ◦ை

No one worries about you like your mother, and when she is gone, the world seems unsafe, things that happen unwieldy. You cannot turn to her anymore, and it changes your life forever. There is no one on earth who knew you from the day you were born; who knew why you cried, or when you'd had enough food; who knew exactly what to say when you were hurting; and who encouraged you to grow a good heart. When that layer goes, whatever is left of your childhood goes with her.

ADRIANA TRIGIANI, WRITER

And it came to me, and I knew what
I had to have before my soul would rest.
I wanted to belong—to belong to my
mother. And in return—I wanted my
mother to belong to me.

୭୧ GLORIA VANDERBILT, WRITER, ACTRESS, AND HEIRESS ୨୧

There is no velvet so soft as a mother's lap, no rose as lovely as her smile, no path so flowery as that imprinted with her footsteps.

ARCHIBALD THOMPSON, WRITER

Everybody knows that a good mother gives her children a feeling of trust and stability. She is their earth. She is the one they can count on for the things that matter most of all. She is their food and their bed and the extra blanket when it grows cold in the night; she is their warmth and their health and their shelter; she is the one they want to be near when they cry. She is the only person in the whole world in a whole lifetime who can be these things to her children. There is no substitute for her. Somehow even her clothes feel different to her children's hands from anybody else's clothes. Only to touch her skirt or her sleeve makes a troubled child feel better.

KATHARINE BUTLER HATHAWAY, WRITER

Mothers were the only ones you
could depend on to tell the whole,
unvarnished truth.

᭦ Margaret Dilloway, writer ᭤

Mother who gave me life, I think of
women bearing women. Forgive me the
wisdom I would not learn from you.

᭦ Gwen Harwood, poet ᭤

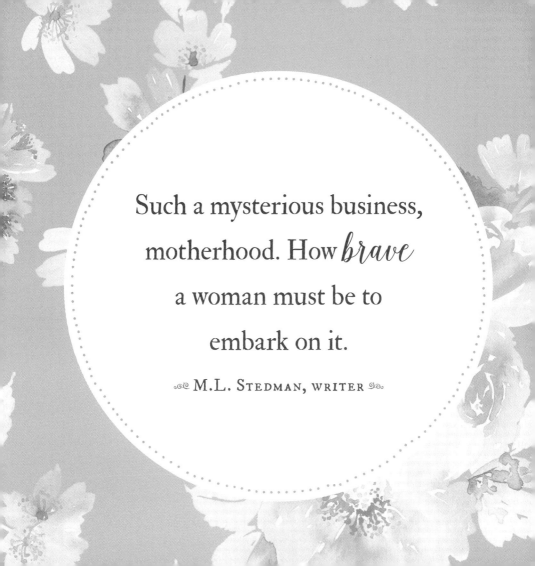

Such a mysterious business, motherhood. How *brave* a woman must be to embark on it.

M.L. STEDMAN, WRITER

Backward, turn backward, O Time, in your flight,

Make me a child again, just for tonight!

Mother, come back from the echoless shore,

Take me again to your heart as of yore;

Kiss from my forehead the furrows of care,

Smooth the few silver threads out of my hair;

Over my slumbers your loving watch keep—

Rock me to sleep, mother—rock me to sleep.

ELIZABETH AKERS ALLEN, WRITER AND JOURNALIST

Being a mother is learning about strengths you didn't know you had, and dealing with fears you didn't know existed.

൦ LINDA WOOTEN, WRITER ൭

My mom's the one I look up to for everything . . . I feel like I'm a lump of clay and she's moulding me into a woman.

CHLOE GRACE MORETZ, ACTRESS

I really learned it all from mothers.

BENJAMIN SPOCK, MD, PEDIATRICIAN AND WRITER

Yes, a mother is one thing that nobody can do without. And when you have harassed her, buffeted her about, tried her patience, and worn her out, and it seems that the end of the world is about to descend upon you, then you can win her back with four little words, "Mom, I love you."

∾ WILLIAM A. GREENBAUM II, WRITER ∾

Motherhood has taught me the *meaning* of living in the moment and being at peace. Children don't think about yesterday, and they don't think about tomorrow. They just exist in the moment.

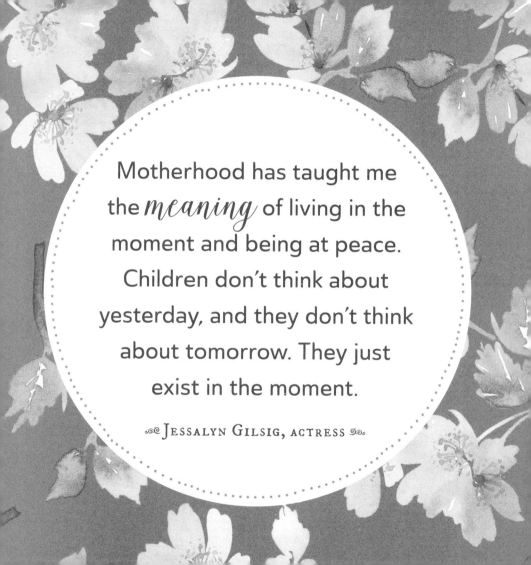

JESSALYN GILSIG, ACTRESS

A mother is she who can take the place of all others, but whose place no one else can take.

෧෬ ANONYMOUS ෨෭

Mother love is the fuel that enables a normal human being to do the impossible.

෧෬ MARION C. GARRETTY, WRITER ෨෭

The most important thing a father can do for his children is to love their mother.

~ THEODORE HESBURGH, FORMER PRESIDENT OF THE UNIVERSITY OF NOTRE DAME ~

My mom is a hard worker. She puts her head down and she gets it done. And she finds a way to have fun. She always says, "Happiness is your own responsibility." That's probably what I quote from her and live by the most.

~ JENNIFER GARNER, ACTRESS ~

This is what we do, my mother's life said. We find ourselves in the sacrifices we make.

๑๑ CAMMIE McGOVERN, WRITER ๑๑

When you're in the thick of raising your kids by yourself, you tend to keep a running list of everything you think you're doing wrong. I recommend taking a lot of family pictures as evidence to the contrary.

๑๑ CONNIE SCHULTZ, WRITER ๑๑

It is clear to me, every little while, that my soul is not big enough to get along without a very personal reason for existence. You will be that person for a long, long time yet. Won't you?

CRYSTAL EASTMAN, LAWYER, ACTIVIST, AND JOURNALIST, TO HER MOTHER, ANNIS FORD EASTMAN

I wonder if my first breath was as soul-stirring to my mother as her last breath was to me.

∽ LISA GOICH, WRITER ∾

A mother is not a person to lean on, but a person to make leaning unnecessary.

∽ DOROTHY CANFIELD FISHER, WRITER AND EDUCATOR ∾

She was such a good loving mother, my best friend.
Oh, who was happier than I when I could still say
the dear name "Mother," and it was heard,
and whom can I say it to now?

～ LUDWIG VAN BEETHOVEN, COMPOSER ～

I would say that my mother is the
single biggest role model in my life,
but that term doesn't seem to encompass
enough when I use it about her.
She was the love of my life.

～ MINDY KALING, ACTRESS ～

At work, you think of the children you've left at home. At home, you think of the work you've left unfinished. Such a struggle is unleashed within yourself. Your heart is rent.

∾ GOLDA MEIR, FORMER PRIME MINISTER OF ISRAEL ∾

Mothers and their children are in a category all their own. There's no bond so strong in the entire world. No love so instantaneous and forgiving.

∾ GAIL TSUKIYAMA, WRITER ∾

It was my mother who taught us to stand up to our problems, not only in the world around us but in ourselves.

෮ DOROTHY PITMAN HUGHES, WRITER AND ACTIVIST ෯

My mother had a slender, small body, but a large heart—a heart so large that everybody's joys found welcome in it, and hospitable accommodation.

෮ MARK TWAIN, WRITER ෯

My mother wasn't what the world would call a good woman. She never said she was. And many people, including the police, said she was a bad woman. But she never agreed with them, and she had a way of lifting up her head when she talked back to them that made me know she was right.

Ben Reitman, Sister of the Road: The Autobiography of Box-Car Bertha

What Mom cares about most is that I'm happy, healthy, and enjoying my life.

Chaz Bono, writer and musician

She looked out into the sunshine. Her full face was not soft; it was controlled, kindly. Her hazel eyes seemed to have experienced all possible tragedy and to have mounted pain and suffering like steps into a high calm and a superhuman understanding. She seemed to know, to accept, to welcome her position, the citadel of the family, the strong place that could not be taken.

JOHN STEINBECK, WRITER

Mothers are
the *necessity*
of invention.

öö BILL WATTERSON, CARTOONIST öö

Anyone who doesn't miss the past never had a mother.

⚬⚬ GREGORY NUNN, ATHLETE ⚬⚬

To describe my mother would be to write about a hurricane in its perfect power.

⚬⚬ MAYA ANGELOU, POET ⚬⚬

Whenever I feel myself inferior to everything about me, threatened by my own mediocrity, frightened by the discovery that a muscle is losing its strength, a desire its power, or a pain the keen edge of its bite, I can still hold up my head and say to myself: . . . "Let me not forget that I am the daughter of a woman who bent her head, trembling, between the blades of a cactus, her wrinkled face full of ecstasy over the promise of a flower, a woman who herself never ceased to flower, untiringly, during three quarters of a century."

⸱⸱ COLETTE, NOVELIST ⸱⸱

The best way to keep children home is to make the home atmosphere pleasant—and let the air out of the tires.

෨෨ DOROTHY PARKER, WRITER ෨෨

Motherhood is not a hobby,
it is a calling. . . . It is not something
to do if you can squeeze the time in.
It is what God gave you time for.

෨෨ RACHEL JANKOVIC, WRITER ෨෨

It's a funny thing about mothers and fathers.
Even when their own child is the most disgusting
little blister you could ever imagine, they still
think that he or she is wonderful.

ഏ ROALD DAHL, WRITER ഏ

I was a Brownie for a day.
My mom made me stop.
She didn't want me to conform.

ഏ SANDRA BULLOCK, ACTRESS ഏ

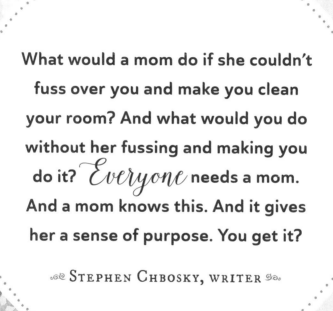

What would a mom do if she couldn't fuss over you and make you clean your room? And what would you do without her fussing and making you do it? *Everyone* needs a mom. And a mom knows this. And it gives her a sense of purpose. You get it?

ॐ STEPHEN CHBOSKY, WRITER ॐ

I wondered if my smile was as big as hers. Maybe as big. But not as beautiful.

⊙ BENJAMIN ALIRE SÁENZ, WRITER ⊙

I looked on child rearing not only as a work of love and duty but as a profession that was fully as interesting and challenging as any honorable profession in the world and one that demanded the best that I could bring to it.

⊙ ROSE KENNEDY, PHILANTHROPIST ⊙

Perhaps you still don't realize . . . how very much
I have admired you: for your work, your teaching,
your strength, and your creation of our exquisite
home . . . I don't think I've ever specifically told you all
that I love and revere, and it is a great, great deal!

～ SYLVIA PLATH, POET ～

These remarkable women of olden times
are like the ancient painted glass—
the art of making them is lost;
my mother was less than her mother,
and I am less than my mother.

～ HARRIET BEECHER STOWE, WRITER AND ABOLITIONIST ～

I like it when my mother smiles. And I especially like it when I make her smile.

ഐ ADRIANA TRIGIANI, WRITER ഇ

Oh, what a power is motherhood, possessing

A potent spell.

All women alike

Fight fiercely for a child.

ഐ EURIPIDES, PLAYWRIGHT ഇ

It wasn't so long ago that I was a working mom myself. And I know that sometimes, much as we all hate to admit it, it's just easier to park the kids in front of the TV for a few hours, so we can pay the bills or do the laundry or just have some peace and quiet for a change.

ᴏᴊᴏ MICHELLE OBAMA, FORMER FIRST LADY OF THE UNITED STATES ᴏᴊᴏ

Because even if the whole world was throwing rocks at you, if you had your mother at your back, you'd be okay. Some deep-rooted part of you would know you were loved. That you deserved to be loved.

ৰ JoJo Moyes, WRITER ৯

I'm a Mommy's Girl—the strongest influence in my young life was my mom.

ৰ Susie Bright, WRITER AND FEMINIST ৯

Completeness? Happiness? These words don't come close to describing my emotions. There truly is nothing I can say to capture what motherhood means to me, particularly given my medical history.

ᨖ ANITA BAKER, MUSICIAN ᨖ

Women as the guardians of children possess great power. They are the molders of their children's personalities and the arbiters of their development.

ᨖ ANN OAKLEY, WRITER AND SOCIOLOGIST ᨖ

Mothers can look
through a child's eyes
and see *tomorrow.*

REED MARKHAM, WRITER AND SPEAKER

My mother is my root, my foundation. She planted the seed that I base my life on, and that is the belief that the ability to achieve starts in your mind.

సౌ MICHAEL JORDAN, FORMER PROFESSIONAL BASKETBALL PLAYER సౌ

Mummy herself has told us that she looked upon us more as her friends than her daughters. Now that is all very fine, but still, a friend can't take a mother's place. I need my mother as an example which I can follow, I want to be able to respect her.

సౌ ANNE FRANK, WRITER సౌ

I cannot forget my mother.
She is my bridge. When I needed to
get across, she steadied herself long
enough for me to run across safely.

᳄ RENITA WEEMS, THEOLOGIAN AND WRITER ᳄

My mother is a woman who speaks
with her life as well as her tongue.

᳄ KESAYA E. NODA, WRITER ᳄

I want to be more successful as a mother than I am in show business.

CELINE DION, MUSICIAN

Sure I love the dear silver that shines in your hair,
And the brow that's all furrowed, and wrinkled with care.
I kiss the dear fingers, so toil-worn for me,
Oh, God bless you and keep you, Mother Machree!

RIDA JOHNSON YOUNG, PLAYWRIGHT AND SONGWRITER

My mom is a never-ending song in my heart of comfort, happiness, and being. I may sometimes forget the words but I always remember the tune.

∽ GRAYCIE HARMON, WRITER ∼

Men are what their mothers made them.

∽ RALPH WALDO EMERSON, POET AND ESSAYIST ∼

Being a mom has made me so tired— and so *happy*.

⁓ TINA FEY, ACTRESS ⁓

Throughout my life, my mom has been the person that I've always looked up to.

ˢ⸙ MIKE KRZYZEWSKI, BASKETBALL COACH ⸙ˢ

A man never sees all that his mother has been to him until it's too late to let her know that he sees it.

ˢ⸙ WILLIAM DEAN HOWELLS, WRITER AND CRITIC ⸙ˢ

The students of history know that while many mothers of great men have been virtuous, none have been commonplace, and few have been happy.

ഔ GERTRUDE ATHERTON, WRITER ൠ

You don't have to be famous. You just have to make your mother and father proud of you.

ഔ MERYL STREEP, ACTRESS ൠ

I know her face by heart.
Sometimes I think nothing
will break her spell.

ཋ Daphne Merkin, literary critic ﰀ

You realize that you habitually thought of Mom when something in your life was not going well, because when you thought of her it was as though something got back on track, and you felt re-energized.

৵ৎ KYUNG-SOOK SHIN, WRITER ৩৹

It is a general rule that all superior men inherit the elements of their superiority from their mothers.

৵ৎ JULES MICHELET, HISTORIAN ৩৹

A Freudian slip is when you say one thing but mean your mother.

ⳉⳁ Anonymous ⳋⳡ

Mothers who have so little sense of their own minds and voices are unable to imagine such capacities in their children. Not being fully aware of the power of words for communicating meaning, they expect their children to know what is on their minds without the benefit of words. These parents do not tell their children what they mean by "good"—much less why. Nor do they ask the children to explain themselves.

ⳉⳁ Mary Field Belenky, professor ⳋⳡ

My favorite thing about being a mom is just what a better person it makes you on a daily basis. Every morning when I wake her up, the endgame is, "Can I get her to smile?" And that puts me in a good mood. It's definitely a different way to live—and a much better one.

ఴఴ DREW BARRYMORE, ACTRESS ఴఴ

When the strongest words for what I have to offer come out of me sounding like words I remember from my mother's mouth, then I either have to reassess the meaning of everything I have to say now, or re-examine the worth of her old words.

৩৫ AUDRE LORDE, WRITER AND ACTIVIST ৩৫

I was always at peace because of the way my mom treated me.

৩৫ MARTINA HINGIS, SWISS PROFESSIONAL TENNIS PLAYER ৩৫

Fortunately, when you're a mom, the responsibility of caring for your child can keep you going.

▪ SHANIA TWAIN, MUSICIAN ▪

Mama was my greatest teacher, a teacher of compassion, love, and fearlessness. If love is sweet as a flower, then my mother is that sweet flower of love.

▪ STEVIE WONDER, MUSICIAN ▪

No song or poem will bear my mother's name. Yet so *many of the stories* that I write, that we all write, are my mother's stories.

ALICE WALKER, WRITER, POET, AND ACTIVIST

Out of the corner of one eye, I could see my mother. Out of the corner of the other eye, I could see her shadow on the wall, cast there by the lamplight. It was a big and solid shadow, and it looked so much like my mother that I became frightened. For I could not be sure whether for the rest of my life I would be able to tell when it was really my mother and when it was really her shadow standing between me and the rest of the world.

◦◦ JAMAICA KINCAID, WRITER ◦◦

In the final analysis, each of us is responsible for what we are. We cannot blame it on our mothers, who, thanks to Freud, have replaced money as the root of all evil.

ﳲ HELEN LAWRENSON, WRITER ﳳ

Sometimes we blame Mom too much for all that is wrong with her sons and daughters. After all, we might well ask, who started the grim mess? Who long ago made Mom and her sex "inferior" and stripped her of her economic and political and sexual rights? . . . Man, born of woman, has found it a hard thing to forgive her for giving him birth. The patriarchal protest against the ancient matriarch has borne strange fruit through the years.

◦◦ LILLIAN SMITH, WRITER ◦◦

I can't help it. I like things clean. Blame it on my mother. I was toilet trained at five months old.

ᏬᏋ Neil Simon, writer ᏋᏬ

I learned your walk, talk, gestures, and nurturing laughter. At that time, Mama, had you swung from bars, I would, to this day, be hopelessly, imitatively, hung up.

ᏬᏋ Diane Bogus, poet ᏋᏬ

Admitting that it is the profession of our sex to teach, we perceive the mother to be first in point of precedence, in degree of power, in the faculty of teaching, and in the department allotted. For in point of precedence she is next to the Creator; in power over her pupil, limitless and without competitor; in faculty of teaching, endowed with the prerogative of a transforming love; while the glorious department allotted is a newly quickened soul and its immortal destiny.

৵৹ে LYDIA HUNTLEY SIGOURNEY, POET ৡ৵৹

The only time a woman really succeeds
in changing a man is when he is a baby.

ᏂᏂ NATALIE WOOD, ACTRESS ᏯᏯ

Becoming a mother makes
you realize you can do almost
anything one-handed.

ᏂᏂ ANONYMOUS ᏯᏯ

I think most women are scared to death, because we are molding and influencing the most important thing we have ever created, our children. So here we are, sailing out into these totally *uncharted waters.* And for someone like me, who was trying and wanting to be the very best at everything, there were a lot of anxious, anxious moments.

ANN RICHARDS, POLITICIAN

[My dad] didn't do much apart from the traditional winning of bread. He didn't take me to get my hair cut or my teeth cleaned; he didn't make the appointments. He didn't shop for my clothes. He didn't make my breakfast, lunch, or dinner. My mother did all of those things, and nobody ever told her when she did them that it made her a good mother.

∽ MICHAEL CHABON, WRITER ∾

I think my mother is my biggest influence. There are so many things I hate about her but at the same time I'm thankful for her. All I know is that when I'm a parent I want to be just like my mom. I can talk to my mom more than any of my friends could talk to their parents.

∽⊗ NIKKI REED, ACTRESS ⊗∾

A woman is her mother.
That's the main thing.

∽⊗ ANNE SEXTON, POET ⊗∾

i am not you anymore i am my own collection of gifts and errors.

ぐ SAUNDRA SHARP, WRITER AND ACTRESS ❧

I can only hope to be 10 percent of the mom mine was to me. She encouraged me to be confident and enjoy life. That's what I want for my son.

ぐ CHARLIZE THERON, ACTRESS ❧

I am a reflection of my mother's secret poetry as well as of her hidden angers.

∾ AUDRE LORDE, WRITER AND ACTIVIST ∾

Even though fathers, grandparents, siblings, memories of ancestors are important agents of socialization, our society focuses on the attributes and characteristics of mothers and teachers and gives them the ultimate responsibility for the child's life chances.

∾ SARA LAWRENCE-LIGHTFOOT, SOCIOLOGIST ∾

When Valentina was not even 1 month old, my aunt [gave me the best advice]: "Put her to sleep yourself every night. Sing to her and cradle her in your arms and sit by her side—every night. Because one day you won't be able to, and it's going to happen really fast."

꧁ SALMA HAYEK, ACTRESS ꧂

Women's rights in essence is really a movement for freedom, a movement for equality, for the dignity of all women, for those who work outside the home and those who dedicate themselves with more altruism than any profession I know to being wives and mothers, cooks and chauffeurs, and child psychologists and loving human beings.

◦◦ JILL RUCKELSHAUS, BUSINESSWOMAN ◦◦

Children are what mothers are.

ⵌ WALTER SAVAGE LANDOR, WRITER ⵌ

I'm still amazed at how my mother emerged from her lonely early life as such an affectionate and levelheaded woman.

ⵌ HILLARY RODHAM CLINTON, FORMER U.S. SECRETARY OF STATE AND U.S. SENATOR ⵌ

A child's hand in yours—what
tenderness and power it arouses.
You are instantly the very touchstone
of wisdom and strength.

⁓ MARJORIE HOLMES, WRITER ⁓

The mother's heart is the
child's schoolroom.

⁓ HENRY WARD BEECHER, CLERGYMAN AND SPEAKER ⁓

Cultural expectations shade and color the images that parents-to-be form. The baby product ads, showing a woman serenely holding her child, looking blissfully and mysteriously contented, or the television parents, wisely and humorously solving problems, influence parents-to-be.

ЕLLEN GALINSKY, PRESIDENT AND COFOUNDER OF THE FAMILIES AND WORK INSTITUTE

What I object to in Mother
is that she wants me to think
her thoughts. Apart from
the question of hypocrisy,
I prefer my own.

❧ MARGARET DELAND, WRITER ☙

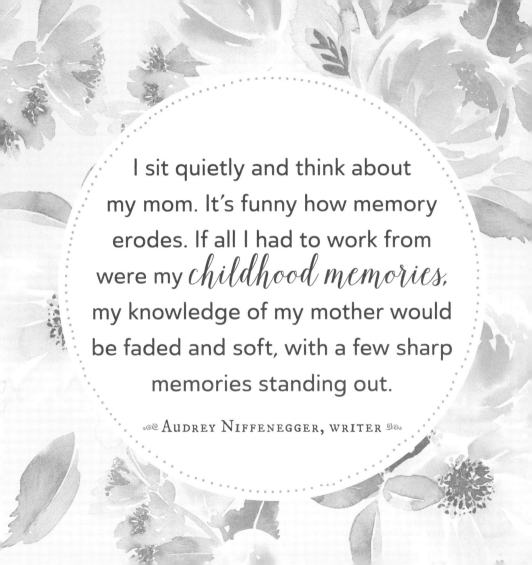

I sit quietly and think about my mom. It's funny how memory erodes. If all I had to work from were my *childhood memories,* my knowledge of my mother would be faded and soft, with a few sharp memories standing out.

⸿ AUDREY NIFFENEGGER, WRITER ⸿

The bond between mothers and their children is one defined by love. As a mother's prayers for her children are unending, so are the wisdom, grace, and strength they provide to their children.

⁂ GEORGE W. BUSH, 43RD PRESIDENT OF THE UNITED STATES ⁂

And prizing more than Plato things I learned
At that best academe, a mother's knee . . .

⁂ JAMES RUSSELL LOWELL, POET, EDITOR, AND DIPLOMAT ⁂

[My son] is at that age now where he's so loving and says the sweetest things to me. Of course, I still get karate chops and all those other sort of things, too.

The death of my mother permanently affects my happiness, more even than I should have anticipated. . . . I did not apprehend, during her life, to what a degree she prevented me from feeling heart-solitude.

ভে SARA COLERIDGE, WRITER ভে

Before you have kids, when you're on a plane and there's a screaming kid, all you can think is, *"Give me earplugs!"* As soon as I became a mom, though, I got it. You find yourself asking, "What can I do? You want me to hold him?" Because you think about the time *your* kid was screaming, and there was the one parent who looked at you and smiled. And that compassion was everything.

శ్రీ MARISKA HARGITAY, ACTRESS ஓ

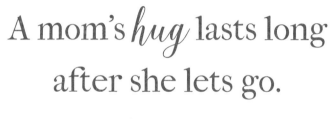

A mom's *hug* lasts long after she lets go.

∞ ANONYMOUS ∞

To say nothing of that brief, but despotic, sway which every woman possesses over the man in love with her—a power immense, unaccountable, incalculable; but in general so evanescent as but to make a brilliant episode in the tale of life—how almost immeasurable is the influence exercised by wives, sisters, friends, and, most of all, by mothers!

～ ANNE MARSH, WRITER ～

You know how parents rattle on to you about, "Oh, you won't believe your life will never be the same," and you think, Why can't these people just get over it? All they're doing is yakking about their kids. It's such a bore. And then you have kids and you just want to do the same thing.

∽ UMA THURMAN, ACTRESS ∼

Any mother could perform the jobs of several air traffic controllers with ease.

LISA ALTHER, WRITER

Yours the voice
Sounding ever in my ears.

MADELEINE MASON-MANHEIM, POET

And so our mothers and grandmothers have, more often than not anonymously, handed on the creative spark, the seed of the flower they themselves never hoped to see; or like a sealed letter they could not plainly read.

ALICE WALKER, WRITER, POET, AND ACTIVIST

Mama exhorted her children at every opportunity to "jump at de sun." We might not land on the sun, but at least we would get off the ground.

༄ ZORA NEALE HURSTON, WRITER AND ANTHROPOLOGIST ༄

If I were asked to define Motherhood,
I would have defined it as Love in its
purest form. Unconditional Love.

෫ Revathi Sankaran, actress ෪

I find, by close observation, that the
mothers are the levers which move in
education. The men talk about it . . . but
the women work most for it.

෫ Frances Watkins Harper, writer and abolitionist ෪

Treetalk and windsong are the language of my mother her music does not leave me.

᠁ BARBARA MAHONE, POET ᠁

I see myself as a mom first. I'm so lucky to have that role in life. The world can like me, hate me, or fall apart around me and at least I wake up with my kids and I'm happy.

᠁ ANGELINA JOLIE, ACTRESS ᠁

The mother's face and voice are the first conscious objects as the infant soul unfolds, and she soon comes to stand in the very place of God to her child.

GRANVILLE STANLEY HALL, PSYCHOLOGIST

I'm simply the mom who makes the lunch, drives to school, finds where the toys are, washes the clothes, and I'm *here to play*. And that's all I should be.

ɷ SANDRA BULLOCK, ACTRESS ɷ

The most universal of truisms is that we all have had a mother. However long or brief that relationship, and however good or bad, there is no disputing that the quality of that relationship is central to our being.

⤚ EMILY ROSEN, WRITER ⤙

Oh, to be only half as wonderful as my child thought I was when he was small, and only half as stupid as my teenager now thinks I am.

⤚ REBECCA RICHARDS, WRITER ⤙

There is no influence
so powerful as that of
the mother.

ༀ SARAH JOSEPHA HALE, WRITER AND EDITOR ༀ

I'm a lioness. I have four cubs.
I'm a mom. I want to take care of
my kids and protect them.

ༀ HEIDI KLUM, MODEL ༀ

I opine . . . "Judicious mothers will always keep in mind, that they are the first book read, and the last put aside, in every child's library."

CHARLES LENOX REMOND, ORATOR AND ABOLITIONIST

What the mother sings to the cradle goes all the way down to the coffin.

HENRY WARD BEECHER, CLERGYMAN AND SPEAKER

I shall never forget my mother, for it was she who planted and nurtured the first seeds of good within me. She opened my heart to the lasting impressions of nature; she awakened my understanding and extended my horizon and her percepts exerted an everlasting influence upon the course of my life.

୭ IMMANUEL KANT, PHILOSOPHER ୭

Having kids—the responsibility of rearing good, kind, ethical, responsible human beings—is the biggest job anyone can embark on. As with any risk, you have to take a leap of faith and ask lots of wonderful people for their help and guidance. I thank God every day for giving me the opportunity to parent.

 මෙ MARIA SHRIVER, JOURNALIST, WRITER, AND FORMER FIRST LADY OF CALIFORNIA ම

I could get away with not taking care of myself as a bachelorette, but as a mom I can't.

ම ALANIS MORISSETTE, MUSICIAN ම

My mother was the making of me. She was so true, so sure of me; and I felt I had someone to live for, someone I must not disappoint. The memory of her will always be a blessing to me.

◦◦ THOMAS EDISON, INVENTOR ◦◦

I've never met a two-year-old who is terrible. I'm so cool with every stage my daughter goes through. I just think *she's amazing.* I hope she's not looking at me thinking, Mom, are the terrible 30s coming on with you?

❧ KATIE HOLMES, ACTRESS ❧

There is something about losing
your mother that is permanent and
inexpressible—a wound that will
never quite heal.

⚜ SUSAN WIGGS, WRITER ⚜

We bear the world, and we make it. . . .
There was never a great man who had
not a great mother—it is hardly an
exaggeration.

⚜ OLIVE SCHREINER, WRITER ⚜

As a mom, you have to look at how much time you're spending with your kids. There is nothing you will regret more in your life—nothing—than not being present for your children.

ぐ♪ JAMIE LEE CURTIS, ACTRESS ♪ぐ

My children are my life. . . . It's not like I don't have my own wants and dreams anymore— it's just that the kids come first.

ぐ♪ ANGIE HARMON, ACTRESS ♪ぐ

Motherhood is the greatest potential influence either for good or ill in human life. . . . It is her caress that first awakens a sense of security; her kiss the first realization of affection; her sympathy and tenderness, the first assurance that there is love in the world. . . . Thus in infancy and childhood she implants ever-directing and restraining influences that remain through life.

ஒ DAVID O. McKAY, 9TH PRESIDENT OF THE CHURCH OF JESUS CHRIST OF LATTER-DAY SAINTS ஒ

And also, one is a mother in order to understand the inexplicable. One is a mother to lighten the darkness. One is a mother to shield when lightning streaks the night, when thunder shakes the earth, when mud bogs one down. One is a mother in order to love without beginning or end.

∾ MARIAMA BA, WRITER ∾

Mother's love grows by giving.

ॐ CHARLES LAMB, WRITER AND ESSAYIST ॐ

My instinct is to protect my children from pain.
But adversity is often the thing that gives us
character and backbone. It's always been
a struggle for me to back off and let my
children go through difficult experiences.

ॐ NICOLE KIDMAN, ACTRESS ॐ

I've learned the value of absorbing the moment.
I remember the first time Ripley saw her shadow.
My God, it was like shadows had just been invented.
It was the most exquisite moment.

ഔ THANDIE NEWTON, ACTRESS ഔ

I've got more children than
I can rightly take care of,
but I ain't got more than
I can love.

ഔ OSSIE GUFFY, WRITER ഔ

She had risen and was walking about the room, her fat, worn face sharpening with a sort of animal alertness into power and protection. The claws that hide in every maternal creature slipped out of the fur of good manners.

∾◦ MARGARET DELAND, WRITER ◦∾

Years to a mother bring distress
But do not make her love the less.

ce WILLIAM WORDSWORTH, POET ɔ

I used to think, What if there's an interesting movie
and it conflicts with the boys going to a new school
for the first time? . . . Well, I didn't anticipate that
was going to be about a two-second dilemma. I didn't
know the choices would be so easy to make.

ce JODIE FOSTER, ACTRESS ɔ

I try to call my mother, Betty, with more regularity because I think, What if Hazel didn't call me for two weeks? I'm *able to see* her mothering now from a different vantage point.

∞ JULIA ROBERTS, ACTRESS ∞

Loving a child doesn't mean giving in to all his whims; to love him is to bring out the best in him, to teach him to love what is difficult.

ഐ NADIA BOULANGER, TEACHER, COMPOSER, AND MUSICIAN ഐ

Love twisted suddenly . . . inside her, compelling her to reach into the crib and lift up the moist, breathing weight. . . . The smells of baby powder and clean skin and warm flannel mingled with a sharp scent of wet nappy.

ഐ ROSIE THOMAS, WRITER ഐ

I'm strict about manners.
I think that kids have a horrible time
with other people if they have bad
manners. . . . The one thing you've got to
be prepared to do as a parent is not
to be liked from time to time.

Emma Thompson, actress

What I think I have in common with every mother on the face of the earth is the primacy of one's children in one's life— that they're everything in some bizarre way.

⋙ JANE SILVERMAN, WRITER ⋘

I got pregnant, and I was like, "Oh God, it worked! Oh no!" [My husband] and I were super happy, then I got terrified! Will I know how to do everything right? Of course, nobody does everything right, but as long as your baby is the priority, that's the best you can do.

⋙ ELLEN POMPEO, ACTRESS ⋘

What do girls do who haven't any mothers to help them through their troubles?

۶۹ LOUISA MAY ALCOTT, WRITER ۶۹

Motherhood has been the most joyous and important experience in my life. I would die for my children.

۶۹ CARLY SIMON, MUSICIAN ۶۹

You were my *home*, Mother. I had no home but you.

JANET FITCH, WRITER

Did you ever meet a mother who's complained that her child phoned her too often? Me neither.

Maureen Lipman, actress

When you are a mother, you are never really alone in your thoughts. You are connected to your child and to all those who touch your lives. A mother always has to think twice, once for herself, and once for her child.

Sophia Loren, actress

Motherhood brings as much joy as ever, but it still brings boredom, exhaustion, and sorrow, too. Nothing else ever will make you as happy or as sad, as proud or as tired, for nothing is quite as hard as helping a person develop his own individuality—especially while you struggle to keep your own.

MARGUERITE KELLY AND ELIA PARSONS, WRITERS

But behind all your stories is always your mother's story, because hers is where yours begin.

MITCH ALBOM, WRITER

My mom had this amazing
attitude in the face of everything,
including when she got cancer.

ဆ BILL CLINTON, 42ND PRESIDENT OF THE UNITED STATES ၆

Becoming a mom to me means you have accepted that
for the next 16 years of your life, you will have a sticky
purse. [Mine] is always filled with stuff I didn't put
there, from leftover Tootsie Rolls to wet wipes that got
squished to the bottom. It makes me laugh every day.

ဆ NIA VARDALOS, ACTRESS ၆

To nourish children and raise them against odds
is in any time, any place, more valuable than to fix
bolts in cars or design nuclear weapons.

೧೬ MARILYN FRENCH, WRITER ೨೦

The mother loves her child most divinely,
not when she surrounds him with comfort
and anticipates his wants, but when
she resolutely holds him to the highest
standards and is content with nothing
less than his best.

೧೬ HAMILTON WRIGHT MABIE, ESSAYIST, EDITOR, AND CRITIC ೨೦

If I get the forty additional years statisticians say are likely coming to me, I could fit in at least one, maybe two new lifetimes. Sad that only one of those lifetimes can include being the mother of young children.

ANNA QUINDLEN, WRITER AND JOURNALIST

[My adopted son] is definitely all mine.
Little souls find their way to you whether
they're from your womb or somebody else's.

ஒ SHERYL CROW, MUSICIAN ஓ

Integral to being emotionally healthy is
to have a mother who has the ability to
respect her child's differences and not
perceive them as betrayals.

ஒ VICTORIA SECUNDA, WRITER ஓ

Probably there is nothing in human nature more resonant with charges than the flow of energy between two biologically alike bodies, one of which has lain in amniotic bliss inside the other, one of which has labored to give birth to the other. The materials are here for the deepest mutuality and the most painful estrangement.

ADRIENNE RICH, WRITER AND FEMINIST

Only a mother knows a mother's fondness.

LADY MARY WORTLEY MONTAGU, ARISTOCRAT AND WRITER

A good mother loves fiercely but ultimately brings up her children to thrive without her. They must be the most important thing in her life, but if she is the most important thing in theirs, she has failed.

ERIN KELLY, WRITER

One surprise of motherhood for me was how little control I have. I thought it would be a blissful romance with me at the helm, cuddling this little creature. It's been bittersweet and humbling to let her lead, and to try not to be perfect myself.

ço Amanda Peet, actress ço

Youth fades, love droops; the leaves of friendship fall:
A mother's secret hope outlives them all.

ৰ৹ OLIVER WENDELL HOLMES, SR., PHYSICIAN AND WRITER ৹ৰ

What I most wanted for my daughter
was that she be able to soar
confidently in her own sky, wherever
that might be, and if there was space
for me as well I would, indeed, have
reaped what I had tried to sow.

ৰ৹ HELEN CLAES, WRITER ৹ৰ

The human heart was not designed to beat outside the human body and yet, each child represented just that— a *parent's heart* bared, beating forever outside its chest.

꧁ DEBRA M. GINSBERG, WRITER ꧂

But the actual power a woman has is to make a group of people happy and make them grow in the right way and contribute to the world. Knowing that you release your family into the day with your love and with your warmth is the richness of life.

ᓚ MARIA SCHELL, ACTRESS ᓗ

It's not our job to toughen our children up to face a cruel and heartless world. It's our job to raise children who will make the world a little less cruel and heartless.

ᨏᨏ L.R. KNOST, WRITER ᨏᨏ

May each of us remember this truth; "one cannot forget mother and remember God. One cannot remember mother and forget God." Why? Because these two sacred persons, God and mother, partners in creation, in love, in sacrifice, in service, are as one.

ᨏᨏ THOMAS S. MONSON, 16TH PRESIDENT OF THE CHURCH OF JESUS CHRIST OF LATTER-DAY SAINTS ᨏᨏ

Despite the happiness which I should have experienced in being away from this place, I cannot consent to separation from [my son]. I could enjoy nothing without my children, and this thought does not leave a regret.

∽ MARIE ANTOINETTE, QUEEN OF FRANCE ∾

[My daughter is] very artistic, but she's also a perfectionist. I feel a little bad: That's the part I see in her that's like me—and you don't want them to have that at age 5.

∽ COURTENEY COX, ACTRESS ∾

Mothers were meant to love us unconditionally, to understand our moments of stupidity, to reprimand us for lame excuses while yet acknowledging our point of view, to weep over our pain and failures as well as cry at our joy and successes, and to cheer us on despite countless start-overs. Heaven knows, no one else will.

৵৹ RICHELLE E. GOODRICH, WRITER ৹৵

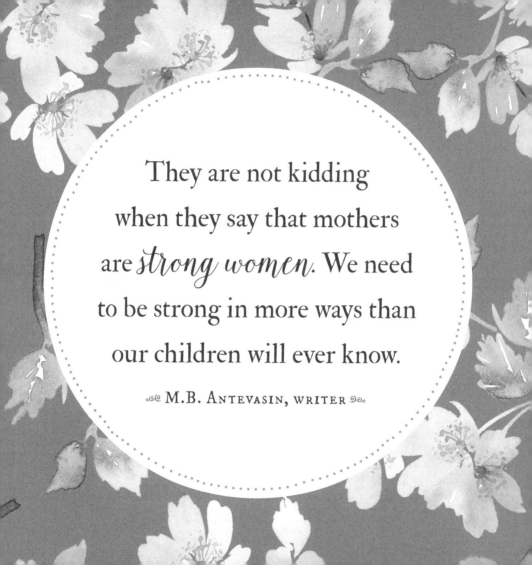

They are not kidding
when they say that mothers
are *strong women*. We need
to be strong in more ways than
our children will ever know.

ঞ M.B. ANTEVASIN, WRITER ঞ

Always that tyrannical love reaches out.

Soft words shrivel me like quicklime.

She will not allow me to be cold, hungry.

She will insist that I take her own coat, her own food.

&ce ELIZABETH SMART, WRITER &&

Being a mother is an attitude, not a
biological relation.

&ce ROBERT A. HEINLEIN, WRITER &&

You never realize how much your mother loves you till you explore the attic—and find every letter you ever sent her, every finger painting, clay pot, bead necklace, Easter chicken, cardboard Santa Claus, paper lace Mother's Day card, and school report since day one.

୭୧ PAM BROWN, POET ୨୧

My parents elected me president of the
family when I was 4. We actually had an election
every year and I always won. I'm an only child,
and I could count on my mother's vote.

ⱰⱰ CONDOLEEZZA RICE, FORMER U.S. SECRETARY OF STATE ⱰⱰ

Romance fails us and so
do friendships, but the relationship
of parent and child, less noisy than
all the others, remains indelible
and indestructible, the strongest
relationship on earth.

ⱰⱰ THEODOR REIK, PSYCHOANALYST ⱰⱰ

A mother's love for her child is like nothing else in the world. It knows no law, no pity. It dares all things and crushes down remorselessly all that stands in its path.

జం AGATHA CHRISTIE, WRITER జం

No one had told her what it would be like, the way she loved her children. What a thing of the body it was, as physically rooted as sexual desire, but without its edge of danger.

ﬔ MARY GORDON, WRITER ﬔ

[A mother's love] is patient and forgiving
when all others are forsaking,
And it never fails or falters
even though the heart is breaking.

HELEN STEINER RICE, POET

For when you looked into my mother's eyes
you knew, as if He had told you, why God
sent her into the world—it was to open the
minds of all who looked to beautiful thoughts.

JAMES M. BARRIE, WRITER

This is a moment that I deeply wish
my parents could have lived to share.
My father would have enjoyed what you
have so generously said of me—and
my mother would have believed it.

ಂ LYNDON B. JOHNSON, 36TH PRESIDENT OF THE
UNITED STATES ಂ

My mother is a walking miracle.

ಂ LEONARDO DICAPRIO, ACTOR ಂ

When my mother had to get dinner for 8 she'd just make enough for 16 and only serve half.

๑๑ GRACIE ALLEN, ACTRESS ๑๑

Before becoming a mother I had a hundred theories on how to bring up children. Now I have seven children and only one theory: love them, especially when they least deserve to be loved.

๑๑ KATE SAMPERI, WRITER ๑๑

Compassion is like mother giving love to her children. Mother's ways are *higher* than others, even when everyone rejects, mother accepts with her arms open and wide.

⊷ AMIT RAY, WRITER ⊶

For that's what a woman, a mother wants—to teach her children to take an interest in life. She knows it's safer for them to be interested in other people's happiness than to believe in their own.

∽ MARGUERITE DURAS, WRITER AND FILMMAKER ∾

. . . There is none,
In all this cold and hollow world, no fount
Of deep, strong, deathless love, save that within
A mother's heart.

∽ FELICIA HEMANS, POET ∾

You made us believe. You kept us off the streets, put clothes on our backs, food on the table. When you didn't eat, you made sure we ate. You went to sleep hungry, you sacrificed for us. You're the real MVP.

KEVIN DURANT, PROFESSIONAL BASKETBALL PLAYER

Mothers are hardest to forgive.
Life is the fruit they long to hand you,
Ripe on a plate. And while you live,
Relentlessly they understand you.

⊛ PHYLLIS McGINLEY, WRITER ⊛

She raised us with humor, and she raised us to understand that not everything was going to be great—but how to laugh through it.

LIZA MINNELLI, SINGER AND ACTRESS

My mother has always been my emotional barometer and my guidance. I was lucky enough to get to have one woman who truly helped me through everything.

&ent; EMMA STONE, ACTRESS &ent;

But all the earth, though it were full of kind hearts, is but a desolation and a desert place to a mother when her only child is absent.

&ent; ELIZABETH GASKELL, WRITER &ent;

My mother said the cure for thinking too much about yourself was helping somebody who was worse off than you.

꧁ SYLVIA PLATH, POET ꧂

Ah, lucky girls who grow up in the shelter of a mother's love—a mother who knows how to contrive opportunities without conceding favors, how to take advantage of propinquity without allowing appetite to be dulled by habit!

꧁ EDITH WHARTON, WRITER ꧂

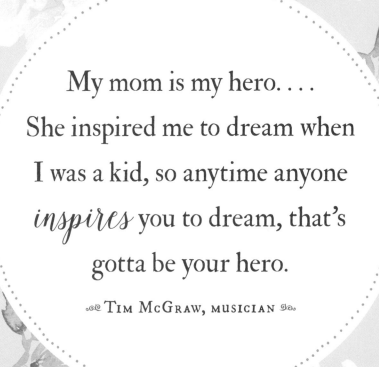

My mom is my hero. . . .
She inspired me to dream when
I was a kid, so anytime anyone
inspires you to dream, that's
gotta be your hero.

✤ TIM McGRAW, MUSICIAN ✤

It has been a terrible, horrible, no good, very bad day. My mom says some days are like that.

ᵍᵉ JUDITH VIORST, WRITER ᵉᵍ

A mother is a person who seeing there are only four pieces of pie for five people, promptly announces she never did care for pie.

ᵍᵉ TENNEVA JORDAN, WRITER ᵉᵍ

Sleep at this point is just
a concept, something
I'm looking forward to
investigating in the future.

෨෨ Amy Poehler, actress ෨෨

It is not until you become a mother
that your judgment slowly turns to
compassion and understanding.

෨෨ Erma Bombeck, humorist ෨෨

You might not have thought it possible to give birth to others before one has given birth to oneself, but I assure you it is quite possible, it has been done; I offer myself in evidence as Exhibit A.

৩๑ SHEILA BALLANTYNE, WRITER ๑๑

My mother was a continual source of wisdom and great advice. She used to say, "Angels fly because they take themselves lightly." And she taught me that there is always a way around a problem—you've just got to find it. Keep trying doors; one will eventually open.

⁖ ARIANNA HUFFINGTON, BUSINESSWOMAN ⁖

As it stands, motherhood is a sort of wilderness through which each woman hacks her way, part martyr, part pioneer; a turn of events from which some women derive feelings of heroism, while others experience a sense of exile from the world they knew.

ജ RACHEL CUSK, WRITER ൭

Life was diapers and little jars of puréed apricots and bottles and playpens and rectal thermometers, and all those small dirty faces and all those questions.

Pat Loud, WRITER

Don't listen to anyone's advice. Listen to your baby. . . . There are so many books, doctors, and well-meaning friends and family. We like to say, "You don't need a book. Your baby is a book. Just pick it up and read it."

Mayim Bialik, ACTRESS

I stood in the hospital corridor the night after she was born. Through a window I could see all the small, crying newborn infants and somewhere among them slept the one who was mine. I stood there for hours filled with happiness until the night nurse sent me to bed.

ಂಲ LIV ULLMANN, ACTRESS ⟡ಲ

Although there are many trial marriages . . . there is no such thing as a trial child.

ಂಲ GAIL SHEEHY, WRITER ⟡ಲ

There is only one pretty child in the world, and every mother has it.

჻ CHINESE PROVERB ჻

I tell my kids,
"I am *thinking* about
you every other
minute of my day."

⚬ MICHELLE OBAMA, FORMER FIRST LADY
OF THE UNITED STATES ⚬

When a child enters the world through you, it alters everything on a psychic, psychological, and purely practical level.

ᗧ JANE FONDA, ACTRESS ᗤ

If you bungle raising your children, I don't think whatever else you do well matters very much.

ᗧ JACQUELINE KENNEDY ONASSIS, FORMER FIRST LADY OF THE UNITED STATES ᗤ

I believe in the strength and intelligence and sensitivity of women. My mother, my sisters—they are strong. My mum is a strong woman and I love her for it.

௸ TOM HIDDLESTON, ACTOR ௸

Five years ago I thought the most courageous thing was not to get married, not to have children. That all seemed so predictable and safe. Now I think the most courageous thing is to get married and have children, because that seems the most worthwhile.

௸ CANDICE BERGEN, ACTRESS ௸

When I pick up one of my children and cuddle them, all the strain and stress of life temporarily disappears. There is nothing more wonderful than motherhood and no-one will ever love you as much as a small child.

⊱ Nicola Horlick, businesswoman ⊰

She's my mom. I'm just unabashedly, unapologetically biased towards her, because I think she's just awesome in every way.

०९ CHELSEA CLINTON, VICE CHAIR OF THE CLINTON FOUNDATION ९०

If you want your children to turn out well, spend twice as much time with them, and half as much money.

०९ ABIGAIL VAN BUREN, COLUMNIST ९०

A mother is always a mother, since a mother is a biological fact, whilst a father is a movable feast.

ᴀɴɢᴇʟᴀ Cᴀʀᴛᴇʀ, ᴡʀɪᴛᴇʀ

To have a son in wartime is the worst curse that can befall a mother, no matter what anyone says.

Sʟᴀᴠᴇɴᴋᴀ Dʀᴀᴋᴜʟɪᴄ, ᴊᴏᴜʀɴᴀʟɪsᴛ

While you can quarrel with a grown-up, how can you quarrel with a newborn baby who has stretched out his little arms for you to pick him up?

இ MARIA VON TRAPP, SINGER ஜ

[My mother] always said I was beautiful and I finally believed her at some point.

இ LUPITA NYONG'O, ACTRESS ஜ

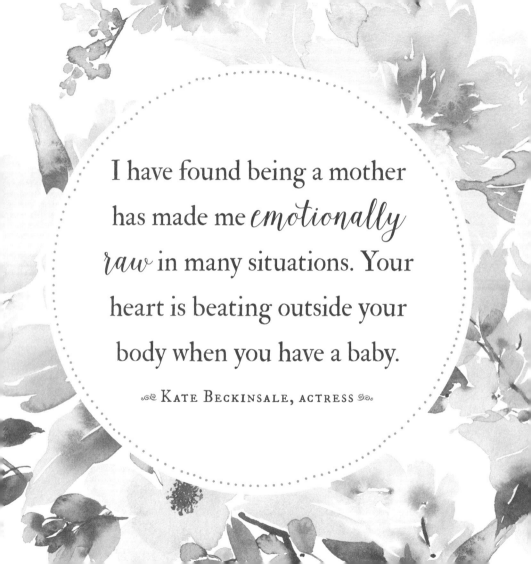

I have found being a mother has made me *emotionally raw* in many situations. Your heart is beating outside your body when you have a baby.

⚬⚬ KATE BECKINSALE, ACTRESS ⚬⚬

My mother was a reader, and she read to us. She read us *Dr. Jekyll and Mr. Hyde* when I was six and my brother was eight; I never forgot it.

ை STEPHEN KING, AUTHOR ை

I've become a mother. That's why women grow up and men don't.

ഏ KATHLEEN CLEAVER, LAW PROFESSOR ഏ

I used to be a reasonably careless and adventurous person before I had children; now I am morbidly obsessed by seat-belts and constantly afraid that low-flying aircraft will drop on my children's school.

ഏ MARGARET DRABBLE, WRITER ഏ

Finally, simply, if I hadn't had a child, I'd never have known that most elemental, direct, true relationship. I don't know if I'd fully understand the values of society that I prize. I would have missed some of the mystery of life and death. Not to know how a child grows, the wonder of a newborn's hand . . . I have been fortunate.

ೋ DIANNE FEINSTEIN, UNITED STATES SENATOR ೕ

Life is crazy. Now, maybe you knew this all along. But before I had children, I actually held on to the illusion that there was some sense of order to the universe. . . . I am now convinced that we are all living in a Chagall painting—a world where brides and grooms and cows and chickens and angels and sneakers are all mixed up together, sometimes floating in the air, sometimes upside down and everywhere.

ᴏᴿ Susan Lapinski, journalist ᴿᴏ

You can't change your mind—you know, and say, this isn't working out, let's sell.

ᴏᴿ Fran Lebowitz, writer, on having children ᴿᴏ

My darling little girl-child, after such a long and troublesome waiting I now have you in my arms. I am alone no more. I have my baby.

ᔆᕫ MARTHA MARTIN, WRITER ᔆᕫ

Children are the anchors that hold a mother to life.

ᔆᕫ SOPHOCLES, GREEK TRAGEDIAN ᔆᕫ

As my mom always said, "You'd rather have smile lines than frown lines."

жж CINDY CRAWFORD, MODEL жж

You are evidence of your mother's strength, especially if you are a rebellious knucklehead and regardless she has always maintained her sanity.

жж CRISS JAMI, WRITER жж

[When] you're dying laughing because your three-year-old made a fart joke, it doesn't matter what else is going on. That's real happiness.

ەﭜﻪ GWYNETH PALTROW, ACTRESS ﻪﭜە

Making the decision to have a child—it is momentous. It is to decide forever to have your heart go walking around outside your body.

ەﭜﻪ ELIZABETH STONE, PROFESSOR AND WRITER ﻪﭜە

Every woman should have a child. The sense of loss must be painful to those without a maternal relationship. You complete the full range of emotions. For me, that's what living is all about.

৩৩ DONNA KARAN, FASHION DESIGNER ৩৩

This is the reason why mothers are more devoted to their children than fathers: it is that they suffer more in giving them birth and are more certain that they are their own.

৩৩ ARISTOTLE, PHILOSOPHER ৩৩

People always talked about a mother's *uncanny ability* to read her children, but that was nothing compared to how children could read their mothers.

ANNE TYLER, WRITER

No woman who understands the gospel would ever think that any other work is more important or would ever say, "I am *just* a mother," for mothers heal the souls of men.

☙ SHERI L. DEW, WRITER ❧

I never get to go to movies,
because I'm a mom.

ᴇᴧ Tɪɴᴀ Fᴇʏ, ᴀᴄᴛʀᴇss ᴀᴇ

We are together, my child and I. Mother
and child, yes, but sisters really, against
whatever denies us all that we are.

ᴇᴧ Aʟɪᴄᴇ Wᴀʟᴋᴇʀ, ᴡʀɪᴛᴇʀ, ᴘᴏᴇᴛ, ᴀɴᴅ ᴀᴄᴛɪᴠɪsᴛ ᴀᴇ

The mother-child relationship is paradoxical and, in a sense, tragic. It requires the most intense love on the mother's side, yet this very love must help the child grow away from the mother, and to become fully independent.

ERICH FROMM, PSYCHOLOGIST

Only mothers can think of the future—because they give birth to it in their children.

MAXIM GORKY, WRITER

No one in the world can take the place of your mother. Right or wrong, from her viewpoint you are always right. She may scold you for little things, but never for the big ones.

ᨀ HARRY TRUMAN, 33RD PRESIDENT OF THE UNITED STATES ᨂ

But now that I'm pregnant I feel beautiful for the first time in my life.

ᨀ KAREN ALEXANDER, MODEL AND ACTRESS ᨂ

I actually remember feeling delight, at two o'clock in the morning, when the baby woke for his feed, because I so longed to have another look at him.

๏ MARGARET DRABBLE, WRITER ๏

The most remarkable thing about my mother is that for thirty years she served the family nothing but leftovers. The original meal has never been found.

ോ CALVIN TRILLIN, WRITER ഌ

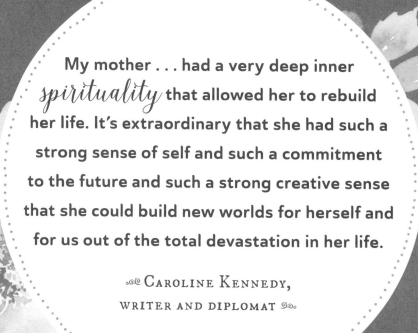

My mother . . . had a very deep inner *spirituality* that allowed her to rebuild her life. It's extraordinary that she had such a strong sense of self and such a commitment to the future and such a strong creative sense that she could build new worlds for herself and for us out of the total devastation in her life.

CAROLINE KENNEDY,
WRITER AND DIPLOMAT

I know how to do anything—
I'm a mom.

ᔥ ROSEANNE BARR, ACTRESS AND WRITER ᔐ

Woman, Mother—your responsibility is
one that might make angels tremble and
fear to take hold!

ᔥ ANNA JULIA COOPER, WRITER ᔐ

Mothers had a thousand thoughts to get through with in a day, and that most of these were about avoiding disaster.

᷈ NATALIE KUSZ, MEMOIRIST ᷈

I love being a mother . . . I am more aware. I feel things on a deeper level. I have a kind of understanding about my body, about being a woman.

᙮ SHELLEY LONG, ACTRESS ᙮

And even if you hate her, can't stand her, even if she's ruining your life, there's something about her, some romance, some power. She's absolutely herself. No matter how hard you try, you'll never get to her. And when she dies, the world will be flat, too simple, reasonable, too fair.

༄ Mona Simpson, writer ༄

Though motherhood is the most important of all the professions—requiring more knowledge than any other department in human affairs—there was no attention given to preparation for this office.

ᏉᏉ ELIZABETH CADY STANTON, SUFFRAGIST ᏉᏉ

Motherhood is the only thing in my life that I've really known for sure is something I wanted to do.

ᏉᏉ CYNTHIA NIXON, ACTRESS ᏉᏉ

There is nothing as sincere
as a mother's kiss.

୬ SALEEM SHARMA, WRITER ୬

God knows that a mother needs fortitude and
courage and tolerance and flexibility and patience and
firmness and nearly every other brave aspect of the
human soul. But because I happen to be a parent of
almost fiercely maternal nature, I praise casualness. It
seems to me the rarest of virtues. It is useful enough
when children are small. It is important to the point of
necessity when they are adolescents.

୬ PHYLLIS MCGINLEY, WRITER ୬

Now, as always, the most automated appliance in a household is the mother.

❧ BEVERLY JONES, FEMINIST ☙

My mother gave me a sense of independence, a sense of total confidence that we could do whatever it was we set out to do. That's how we were raised.

❧ ROBIN WRIGHT, ACTRESS ☙

I was raised by a single mother who made a way for me. She used to scrub floors as a domestic worker, put a cleaning rag in her pocketbook, and ride the subways in Brooklyn so I would have food on the table. But she taught me as I walked her to the subway that life is about not where you start, but where you're going. That's family values.

৩৫ AL SHARPTON, CIVIL RIGHTS ACTIVIST ৩৩

Becoming a mother makes you the mother *of all children*. From now on each wounded, abandoned, frightened child is yours. You live in the suffering mothers of every race and creed and weep with them. You long to comfort all who are desolate.

∾ CHARLOTTE GRAY, WRITER ∾

I'm living proof it's possible to flunk Home Ec, as I did in the eighth grade, and still be an outstanding mother.

ঌ PAT COLLINS, WRITER AND FILM CRITIC ঌ

What is free time? I'm a single mother. My free moments are filled with loving my little girl.

ঌ ROMA DOWNEY, ACTRESS ঌ

Many people have said to me, "What a pity you had such a big family to raise. Think of the novels and the short stories and the poems you never had time to write because of that." And I looked at my children and I said, "These are my poems. These are my short stories."

ॐ OLGA MASTERS, WRITER ॐ

No ordinary work done by man is either as hard or as responsible as the work of a woman who is bringing up a family of small children; for upon her time and strength demands are made not only every hour of the day, but often every hour of the night.

ॐ THEODORE ROOSEVELT, 26TH PRESIDENT OF THE UNITED STATES ॐ

Insanity is hereditary; you get it from your children.

ဆ⌖ SAM LEVENSON, HUMORIST AND TELEVISION PERSONALITY ⌖ఴ

I went to bed feeling melancholy, wishing I could have poured out all my fears and insecurities to my mom. Wasn't that what normal mothers and daughters did?

ဆ⌖ RICHELLE MEAD, WRITER ⌖ఴ

Giving kids clothes and food is one thing, but it's much more important to teach them that other people besides themselves are important, and that the best thing they can do with their lives is to use them in the service of other people.

ⁿ⁶ DOLORES HUERTA, LABOR LEADER ⁶ⁿ

Because I am a mother,
I am capable of being shocked;
as I never was when
I was not one.

๑๛ MARGARET ATWOOD, WRITER ๛๑

Mothers hold their children's hands for a
short while, but their hearts forever.

๑๛ ANONYMOUS ๛๑

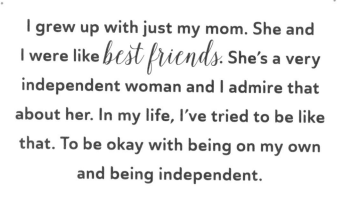

I grew up with just my mom. She and I were like *best friends*. She's a very independent woman and I admire that about her. In my life, I've tried to be like that. To be okay with being on my own and being independent.

&ఎ EMMA ROBERTS, ACTRESS ఇ&

There are lots of things that you can brush under the carpet about yourself until you're faced with somebody whose needs won't be put off.

∽ ANGELA CARTER, WRITER ∾

[Motherhood is] the biggest gamble in the world. It is the glorious life force. It's huge and scary—it's an act of infinite optimism.

∽ GILDA RADNER, ACTRESS ∾

A suburban mother's role is to deliver children obstetrically once, and by car forever after.

ை PETER DE VRIES, EDITOR AND NOVELIST ஒ

I always brought up my children not to believe in Mother's Day gifts, and now I regret it.

ை LAUREN BACALL, ACTRESS AND SINGER ஒ

My mother had died when I was seven.
For many years I lived primarily
to search for her.

∽ JANE LAZARRE, WRITER ∾

Time is the only comforter
for the loss of a mother.

∽ JANE WELSH CARLYLE, RENOWNED LETTER WRITER, WIFE
OF WRITER AND HISTORIAN THOMAS CARLYLE ∾

Mothers may still want their favorite son to grow up to be President but, according to a famous Gallup poll of some years ago, they do not want them to become politicians in the process.

⧼ JOHN F. KENNEDY, 35TH PRESIDENT OF THE UNITED STATES ⧽

The easiest way to convince my kids that they don't really need something is to get it for them.

꧁ JOAN COLLINS, ACTRESS ꧂

For me, it's not the voice of an actress. What I hear is the woman who nursed me through ear infections or told me stories when I was young. It's very unnerving sometimes.

꧁ SEAN FERRER, SON OF AUDREY HEPBURN ꧂

Cleaning your house while your kids are still growing is like shoveling the walk before it stops snowing.

ༀ PHYLLIS DILLER, ACTRESS AND COMEDIAN ༀ

Motherhood is like Albania— you can't trust the descriptions in the books, you have to go there.

ༀ MARNI JACKSON, WRITER ༀ

The darn trouble with cleaning the house is it gets dirty the next day anyway, so *skip a week* if you have to. The children are the most important thing.

BARBARA BUSH, FORMER FIRST LADY
OF THE UNITED STATES

I am sure that if the mothers
of various nations could meet,
there would be no more wars.

∞ E.M. FORSTER, WRITER ∞

That strong mother doesn't tell her cub, Son, stay
weak so the wolves can get you. She says, Toughen
up, this is reality we are living in.

∞ LAURYN HILL, MUSICIAN ∞

Mama took me in her arms and held me tight. Her embrace was hot and she smelled like sweat, dust, and grease, but I wanted her. I wanted to crawl inside her mind to find that place that let her smile and sing through the worst dust storms. If I had to be crazy, I wanted my mama's kind of crazy, because she was never afraid.

୶ SARAH ZETTEL, WRITER ଖ

Motherhood is a wonderful thing—what a pity to waste it on children.

⁓ JUDITH PUGH, WRITER ⁓

As far as I'm concerned, there's no job more important on the planet than being a mom.

⁓ MARK WAHLBERG, ACTOR ⁓

Over the years I have learned that motherhood is much like an austere religious order, the joining of which obligates one to relinquish all claims to personal possessions.

∞ NANCY STAHL, ILLUSTRATOR ∞

I'm really clear about my priority in life—it's being a mom . . . I love doing films, but I wouldn't like to do that more than I'd like to be my daughter's mother.

∞ TERI HATCHER, ACTRESS ∞

Motherhood is not for the faint-hearted. Frogs, skinned knees, and the insults of teenage girls are not meant for the wimpy.

ॐ DANIELLE STEEL, WRITER ॐ

Motherhood in all its guises and permutations is more art than science.

ॐ MELINDA M. MARSHALL, WRITER ॐ

SOURCES

About.com: http://womenshistory.about
.com/od/motherhood/a/mother_quotes
.htm

BrainyQuote.com: www.brainyquote.com/
quotes/keywords/motherhood.html

Buzzfeed: https://www.buzzfeed.com/
jarrylee/beautiful-quotes-for-mothers-
day?utm_term=.vgXx81yWV#.hrKXQ6Mzw

ESPN: www.espn.com/espn/page2/
index?id=5175180

Glamumous: www.glamumous.co.uk/
2013/05/50-literary-quotes-about-mothers
.html

Good Housekeeping: www.goodhouse
keeping.com/life/inspirational-stories/
interviews/g1694/celebrity-moms/?slide=1

Goodreads.com: www.goodreads.com/
quotes/tag/motherhood?page=1

Huffington Post: www.huffingtonpost
.ca/2014/04/21/mothers-day-quotes_n_
5188234.html

Inquisitr.com: www.inquisitr.com/2079207/
mothers-day-quotes-31-of-the-funniest-
sweetest-cleverest-and-truest-mothers-day-
quotes/

Modern Mama: http://modernmama.com/
blog/2013/02/25/best-motherhood-quotes/

Mom Junction: www.momjunction.com/
articles/top-100-quotes-mother_006643/

Momscape.com: www.momscape.com/
articles/mother-quotes.htm

Mormon.org: https://www.mormon.org/
blog/100-inspiring-quotes-about-being-a-
mother

MothersDayCelebration.com: http://www
.mothersdaycelebration.com/twenty-
mothers-day-quotes.html

Parade.com: http://parade.com/288611/
viannguyen/100-inspiring-quotes-about-
moms-for-100-years-of-mothers-day/3/

People: http://celebritybabies.people.com/
2008/01/05/mia-hamm/

ProFlowers.com: /www.proflowers.com/
blog/80-mothers-day-quotes

Psychology Today: https://www.psychology
today.com/blog/here-there-and-
everywhere/201205/50-quotes-mothers

QuoteGarden.com: www.quotegarden
.com/mothers.html

Searchquotes.com: www.searchquotes
.com/quotation/I_was_always_at_peace_
because_of_the_way_my_mom_treated_
me./118386/

TheFreshQuotes.com: www.thefreshquotes
.com/mothers/

Today's Parent: www.todaysparent.com/
blogs/celebrity-candy/celebrity-moms-
motherhood/